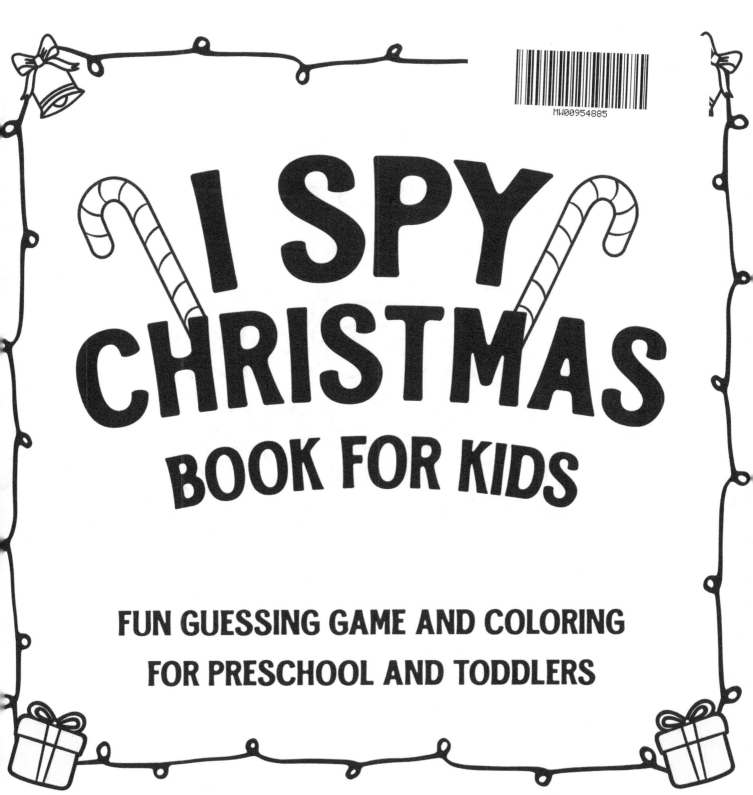

I SPY CHRISTMAS
BOOK FOR KIDS

**FUN GUESSING GAME AND COLORING
FOR PRESCHOOL AND TODDLERS**

ALL PAGES CAN BE COLORED IN FOR EXTRA FUN!

THIS BOOK BELONGS TO:

ANGEL

BELL

CANDY

I SPY WITH MY LITTLE EYE SOMETHING STARTING WITH...

D

DOG

ELF

FIREPLACE

GINGERBREAD

I SPY WITH MY LITTLE EYE SOMETHING STARTING WITH...

HAT

I SPY WITH MY LITTLE EYE SOMETHING STARTING WITH...

IGLOO

I SPY WITH MY LITTLE EYE SOMETHING STARTING WITH...

JINGLE BELLS

KEY

I SPY WITH MY LITTLE EYE SOMETHING STARTING WITH...

LIGHTS

MITTENS

NUTCRACKER

I SPY WITH MY LITTLE EYE SOMETHING STARTING WITH...

ORNAMENT

I SPY WITH MY LITTLE EYE
SOMETHING STARTING WITH...

PENGUIN

I SPY WITH MY LITTLE EYE SOMETHING STARTING WITH...

QUEEN

REINDEER

I SPY WITH MY LITTLE EYE
SOMETHING STARTING WITH...

SNOWMAN

I SPY WITH MY LITTLE EYE SOMETHING STARTING WITH...

TREE

I SPY WITH MY LITTLE EYE SOMETHING STARTING WITH...

UMBRELLA

I SPY WITH MY LITTLE EYE SOMETHING STARTING WITH...

VASE

I SPY WITH MY LITTLE EYE
SOMETHING STARTING WITH...

W O

WREATH

I SPY WITH MY LITTLE EYE SOMETHING STARTING WITH...

XYLOPHONE

I SPY WITH MY LITTLE EYE SOMETHING STARTING WITH...

YULE LOG

I SPY WITH MY LITTLE EYE SOMETHING STARTING WITH...

ZERO

Made in the USA
Las Vegas, NV
06 November 2024

11178761R00059